as i learnt to fly

As I Learnt to Fly
Print Edition

First Published in India in 2020
Inkfeathers Publishing
New Delhi 110095

ISBN 978-81-948219-8-4

Edited by Tanishk Singh

www.inkfeathers.com

as i learnt to fly

A plethora of perennial verses

Edited & Compiled by

Tanishk Singh

Inkfeathers Publishing

DISCLAIMER

The anthology "As I learnt to fly" is a collection of poems by 26 authors who belong to different parts of the globe. The anthology editor and the publisher have edited the content provided by the co-authors to enhance the experience for readers and make it free of plagiarism as much as possible. The poems published in this book are solely owned by their respective authors. In case, any sort of plagiarism is detected in the poems within this anthology or in case of any complaints or grievances or objections, neither the anthology editor, nor the publisher are to be held responsible for any such claims. The author(s) who holds the rights to the particular poem(s), shall be held responsible, whatsoever.

CO-AUTHORED BY

Bhavya Rao ~ Pooja Shroff ~ Sanyogita Bharadwaj ~

Arubah Nadeem ~ Tanvi Kulkarni ~ Arati Harikumar ~

Sarah Kordos ~ Priyanka Ravi Nair ~ Kunika Rawlani ~

Sree Yelamanchi ~ Sneha Hembram ~ Amol Gawade ~

Khushi Thakare ~ Maria Wynnyckyj ~ Frances Abhulimen ~

Affan Alam ~ Afreen Fatima ~ C.L. Williams ~ Jagruthi Kommuri ~

Namita Das ~ Dr. Apteena Johnson Kakkadu ~ Rajlakshmi Kurup ~

Ashwini Pandit ~ Pravallika Kadiri ~ Anushree Gupta ~

Snehal Agarwal

CONTENTS

ABOUT THE EDITOR

TANISHK SINGH

Tanishk is a 20-year-old literature and music enthusiast who likes to crack lame jokes and sometimes, cook. His thought process is as disjointed as the lines above and he believes in writing what he thinks. He's a singer, songwriter, and a guitarist to boot. He's composed a few unreleased songs and plans on releasing them soon. Already the editor of an anthology available worldwide, he wishes to pursue all that he thinks is interesting.

You can follow him on Instagram @half_guitarist.

EDITOR'S NOTE

I searched on google "what is an editor's note", and got a very profound and meaningful answer, which was: "an editor's note is a note written by the editor".
Very profound and meaningful right? No. Not at all, but that doesn't matter. Now that I have your attention, let me begin the actual note.

Compiling the book was a rough task, but what gave me the most pleasure while doing so was reading through all the entries we received for the book. Each of them was unique and told their own stories, expressing their own emotions. Since the theme was 'a random collection of poetry', we received a plethora of genres of poetry, ranging from romantic to tragic, from all over the world. Staying true to the theme of the book, I've compiled all the poetry randomly. Yes, you read that right. Randomly.

You won't know when a poem will make you go soft in your heart and when one will shatter your fragile soul in a million pieces. You won't know when a poem will take you on a joyride and when it'll become a nightmare, and that is what will probably drive you to keep flipping the pages and read the book from the start to the finish in one go.

Although I'll recommend you to randomly open any page in the book and read a poem, it's your call.

For a note this has become quite long so now I'll take your (metaphorical) leave and I hope you enjoy this collection!

-Tanishk Singh

as i learnt to fly

TRY

Those little fingers all tired and timid
Those little crushed papers surrounding the bin
Those unwashed coffee mugs with
Those last few drops left almost drying
Those little thoughts in your mind still fighting
That little brain still processing
That little heart still racing
Ooh little child
I know it's hard
I know your arms hurt
I know your nerves are giving up
I know you think it's over
But do you think all this pain was worth not trying
another shot of that expresso with
Bitter taste just like life and yet not giving up
As the heat kept you going
I hope you keep trying

-Bhavya Rao

STRANGER WITH YELLOW UMBRELLA

In a long winter night,
In a long sad night,
In a long milky night,
I think of you
With a sad heart
Stranger with yellow umbrella,
I think of you.

In a long summer night,
In a long dizzy day,
In a sad autumn noon,
You cross my mind
With a sad smile
Stranger with yellow umbrella,
You cross my mind.

In a blurry rainy day,
In a hazy rainy street,
In a long passing night,
Without that yellow umbrella
You disappear in a blue night

In a sulky starry night,
In a dusky moon night,
I leave you as a stranger,
With a cloudy heart
I leave you as a stranger,
Stranger with yellow umbrella.

-Pooja Shroff

CALMING TRUTH

Tonight,

I'll tell you the scariest thing.

It's dark. It probably will be for quite a while.

But

You can still stay though.

You can keep on with a smile, I swear all this struggle will be

worthwhile.

By time you'll shine.

And right now, I'll tell you the most beautiful thing?

Amidst this darkness you'll shine.

You'll be the sunshine.

It's just about time.

It'll be yours in no time.

So, don't worry. I know it's dark, but you'll soon shine.

-Sanyogita Bharadwaj

MEMORIES

You showed me the love and care that I have never seen or received

from anybody with such delicacy

Of all the people,

You told me nobody would love me the way you did

You told me nobody would trust me the way you did

You told me I would never be able to find my way ever again

You told me I would never be able to give my everything to the

people I love

But I hope and pray that's not true even in the slightest way possible.

I hope to find all of those things you made me believe I would never

receive or ever be capable enough to give others in return.

-Arubah Nadeem

DESIRE

Just wanted to fade
dissolve
be lost in the depth
far
disappear in the crowd
invisible

This world isn't worth your worry, sadness, jealousy, hatred
A fighter will also be the one trying till the end no matter how
drastically everything changes in life.
And a soldier will always protect anybody they have to.

-Arubah Nadeem

ALL I DID WAS LEAVE

It was that one lonely night
When I had this subtle thoughts of
human existence
Different perceptions
Cross genders
Undefined sex
Polluted weather
And all at once it occurred that nothing mattered because every time
I thought of any of it all I could remember was
what's the purpose of my existence if you weren't beside,
Why is that we had different perceptions that could never meet
Why is that you had to feel the same love for someone like you
Was all the time we made love a whole lie and can never be defined?
And then you left me in this agony where I kept polluting my
thoughts, lungs, liver and now the weather too.
This was enough irrelevant pain I had experienced because nobody
could change the way you were born nor the way I felt for you so all I
did was leave

-Bhavya Rao

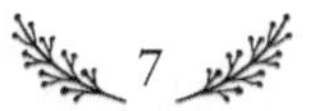

BEYOND FAITH

I lay here today shivering

no one to help me with it because it's one of those days which I can

surely explain but words may not come out of my mouth.

I feel empty but I'm not lonely

I feel the cold like I have never felt before

I feel l might break

but that's not what I want

Not today and especially not right now,

because I know I won't be able to hide the fear and pain in me if I

break

I can't and I hope I don't.

-Arubah Nadeem

FOOTPRINTS

Has anyone seen,
Little footprints so keen,
On the sandy shore,
Where wind blows galore.

Inquisitive footprints that freely ambled,
Near the lowly hut that was in shambles,
Running along the shoreline,
A pair of which were mine.

Mine, or were they figments?
Of imagination's colourful pigments,
Washed away by the waves that rushed,
Memories that got shushed.

Shushed, but now waking,
Is that a cuckoo singing?
I swear there is no change,
In its melodious vocal range.

Change I do observe,
In the memories I now conserve,
Gone are the happy footprints,
Replaced by ambitious newspaper prints.

Prints bearing the works,
Of those dining with fine forks,
And silver-plated knives,
While the ordinary crowd like beehives.

Hives of confines,
Social and mental fake "I'm fines",
Strangling of fictional aspirations,
By the grim factual realizations.

How will justice reach the strangled?
Restore the lost empathy to those entangled,
In society's fake strings,
Of the futile pampering.

My mirror tells,
Break out of such spells,
Look at yourself in the present,
You're yet not decadent.

You have time to revert,

From the corrupt,

Return is priced at zero dimes,

Just follow those little footprints on the sands of times

-Tanvi Kulkarni

BELIEVE

If there is one thing you must do, always and forever till your
breath leaves you is to Believe...

Believe that the best is yet to come and that the rays of the sun
shine solely for you
Believe that the world is beautiful, sacred place and that you are
blessed to be a part of this cosmos
Believe that everything that happens for a reason is only to lead
you to your destiny
Believe that you are magical and that the universe always has her
grace on you
Believe that you are stronger and wiser than yesterday and love
the lessons it has taught you
Believe in goodness for this has never failed a soul

Believe that this belief will guide you today, tomorrow, always
and forever....
If there is one thing you must do, is to always believe

-Arati Harikumar

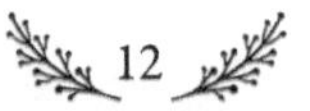

AMIDST NOWHERE

Those deserted footprints will tell you a story,
Listen carefully to what they have to say

Those birds that soar high will tell you a story,
Listen carefully to their chirping

The winds always carry a message,
Understand their language as they say.

The roots of trees have witnessed many a stories,
Listen to their anguish night and day.

The river that flows by has her turbulence to share,
Open your heart and listen to what she has to say.

The sun when he rises and when he sets,
Has witnessed many miracles in his own way,
Pause and listen to what he has to say.

The moon light shimmers in her beauty hiding some dark secrets
deep within,
Seek her out and probe her further to understand what she has to
say.

The stars that shine on you, teasing you all along,
Laugh along them and listen to what they have to say.

You may learn from them or you may not for what you gain is all
what you seek,
Seek them while you can still breathe.....

-Arati Harikumar

INVALID REPLACEMENT

Let's try and forget the inside jokes that we shared,

the weird funny videos,

those lovely cute baby pictures,

screenshots of our social media from 2013,

hours long phone calls, every birthday picture with cake smeared on

faces,

car rides, weird and disgusting conversations.

God there was so much more than that.

Now where does forgetting it leave you? Nowhere.

You think and pretend that maybe

just maybe

if you forgot all the good and bad memories that you shared,

you will most probably be happy because

there won't be any pain left to feel

But that also leaves you to be entirely empty.

So don't ever tell somebody to try to forget the moments

that are keeping them alive even till today.

-Arubah Nadeem

HER HEART, RUBY RED

the red rose she holds is buried deep –
but its thorns, they stick out strong.

(she's soft, carefree, and so unique.
but deep down, there's something wrong.)

her heart, ruby red, is as fragile as a rose –
therefore, she holds it with such care.

but she's scared her rose will wilt before
it's had a chance to be shared.

-Sarah Kordos

ALIVE IN LOVE

I am so lucky to have this life,
So lucky to be able to feel you.

I feel so lucky to see the morning sun,
So lucky to see the gleaming dew.

Happiness is a choice they say,
And love happens only once.

Well I've chosen to live a happy life
By falling for you and no other one.

-Priyanka Ravi Nair

DANDELION

Like a dandelion
adrift in the wind
sighted,
admired,
applauded,
yet, ignored!!

-Sree Yelamanchi

THE PART OF ME

The part of me is
Still craving for your love

My heart is only
Crying out your name

I know you won't return
Since you never ever

Wanted to be
Part of me

I understand it but,
Something inside me doesn't.

-Sneha Hembram

STAR GAZING

if you've never sat amongst the stars
and stared peacefully into their space,
hands holding you in place
on the grass, on top of a hill,

and you don't start to wonder where you are
or what's around you and how far
you are from knowing
the truth beyond your gaze –

then are you truly living,
or just living out your days?

-Sarah Kordos

SELF-LOVE

Many say self-love is the process of loving yourself,
Wait; do we hate ourselves?

We are not born either with hate or love for ourselves,
Since birth we love Mom, dad, and siblings, maybe we forget
ourselves.

It's a simple act of putting yourself first before anyone else,
And it's not being heedless.

It's healing yourself first,
It's saying yes if you want to,
And not apologizing for not doing something you actually didn't
want to.

Self-love is accepting yourself the way you are,
Embracing it and loving like you love your loved ones.

Self-love is doing what is right for yourself,
Not what you enjoy the most.
(They differ sometimes)

Self-love is taking responsibility of your happiness,
And not blaming or depending on anyone else.

Self-love is not being selfish,
When you love yourself,
You teach others to love themselves too.

-Kunika Rawlani

INSOMNIA

Until then,
Treasure your eyes with truth,
Treasure your diary with pain,
Treasure your heart with memories,
One day,
Sleep would betide but
Treasure your life,
Until then!!

-Sree Yelamanchi

LIFEGUARD

Blood runs through my veins,
My heart sings to its patterned beats
My eyes watch a million different colours,
Both as dark as the night sky
And as bright as the morning sun's glee.

I wake up with a purpose,
A purpose to be of use.
To be able to touch lives in ways unimaginable,
Oh what a lovely mission to pursue!

Being different isn't easy,
Let alone making a difference.
When all people are focused on
Is the fake smile instead of the real pain within.

Save a life, save a generation,
Save a smile from turning into a frown.
If happiness is a real choice,
Let's make it available for everyone.

-Priyanka Ravi Nair

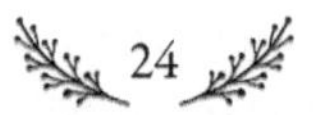

THE QUEST

Wandered through the streets
of lost love,
Plunged deep into the sea
of ruthless reality,
Dived into the sky
of brazen betrayal,
Pondered over the path
of wilted wishes,
Only to
find Myself again

-Sree Yelamanchi

WOUNDED WINGS

There I am "caged",
in a rusted crate,
trying to flee and fly high free,
wishing my flutter pree..
I opened my eyes to see,
my wings buried under a tree..
I closed back my eyes,
hoping it all be a dream of reeds!!

-Sree Yelamanchi

YOU PLAYED WELL

I knew you were a player
Yet I fell for you...

Since my heart was not a player
But you were

You played well
With my feelings

& Trust which I
Bestowed upon you

I trusted
Your faking ploy.

-Sneha Hembram

WHAT HURTS MORE?

Broken ribs or Broken promises?
Bleeding wrists or Bleeding heart?
Blackened eye or Blackened soul?
Strangled neck or Strangled dreams?
Wounded lips or Wounded love?

What hurts more?

-Sree Yelamanchi

VOICELESS LOVE

Walking down the path
our eyes met
Yet she didn't speak and
neither did I...
She couldn't lower her gaze,
neither could I...
Our hearts stumbled on one hope,
either I would speak, or she would...
Yet it didn't upset her and
Neither did it angered me...
I couldn't stand letting her hang onto a single hope..
Long after, suddenly we meet again...
This time she doesn't see me
and neither do I stop to see her...
I would promise my heart to speak to her whenever I saw her...
But neither does she listens,
nor do I speak...
One thing was for sure
that our love was true
And still yet she doesn't deny
Nor do I express...

-Amol Gawade

UNREAL FUTURE

A little moon shine on my eyes,
tingling touch of the drizzly grass,
unvoiced melody of the wind,
flowers giggling around the lake,
falling leaves waving towards you,
And in the Unreal future,
Walking down the hill,
Tweaking the roadside poppies,
Touching the blooming woody plants,
Hearing the unknown night,
Loving the sleety wind,
Picking the fallen cherries,
Holding your purple hat,
Became my real now.

-Pooja Shroff

AS I WAS LEARNING TO FLY

you ignited a flame
and let it blow away with the wind.
you built me up
only to knock me down again.

you gave me wings
with your beautiful lies,
and then tore me down
as I was learning to fly.

I was carelessly thrown
into the cerulean sky,
and with your eyes wide open,
you took away my height.

-Sarah Kordos

EMBROIDERED STARLIGHT

Misty first light,
Chirping cuckoos,
Splashing silver lake,
Lazy winter evenings,
Embroidered starlight,
Warm coffee nights
Old radio songs,
Alleviates my restless heart.

-Pooja Shroff

IN THE GARDEN OF THORNS

She bloomed,
in the tears of rain,
She shined,
in the shades of moon,
She smiled,
in the cries of night,
She sparkled,
in the colours of twilight,
She lived,
in the garden of thorns.

-Pooja Shroff

HIDDEN MOON

Some days,

you are more lucid,

Some nights,

you are less sullen,

Some days,

you are more in my eyes,

Some nights,

you are less in my tears,

Some days,

you are more in my poems,

Some nights,

you are less in my stories,

Some days,

i search for my hidden moon,

Some nights,

I search for my lost wind.

-Pooja Shroff

DISTANCE

So far, yet the sky sees its reflection in oceans, ponds, seas and rivers.
Could be so distant but yet one would mirror their love for one.
The thought itself gives shivers.
How's love so strong? That one sees their own reflection in another
while we all are unique from one another?
Maybe the sky yearns to meet the still waters.
But maybe they're good far off, knowing that the other one is fine and
well.
Although there's a lot to tell.
Maybe, at times love is enough to give you enough strength to stay
away from your loved one. Yet know that you shall always remain
one.

-Sanyogita Bharadwaj

SOMETIMES…SOMEDAY…

Sometimes…someday…
Sit at the window staring at the stars,
Think about life you've lived and spent your hours
Let those cold thoughts tremble your soul,
With a warm blanket for you to wrap and roll.

Sometimes…someday…
Pause the world play and greet yourself,
Forget the fanciness and feel each of your cells.
Assume the stars are twinkling for your smile,
Dark is the night just for you to shine.

Sometimes…someday…
Get a cup of coffee dreaming of your fantasies,
Believe your presence shall affect these galaxies.
Experience the stillness in that dim moonlight,
Peep into the world which was always out of your sight.

Sometimes…someday…
Feel good to be self-obsessed,
You're precious, never think you're messed.

Breathing in royalty breath out the toxicity,
The next morning you'll respect your kindness and simplicity...

That time...that day...
You'll know your authenticity...
That time... that day...
You'll surely know your authenticity...!

-Khushi Thakare

REALIZATIONS

It's always in your most poignant moments, reality hits you
Like a thunderstorm.
You lose your balance, the ground beneath you is shaken.
But you regain yourself,
Little by little.
And in those few moments,
Everything has changed
You are different and what you perceive is not what it used to be.
No one understands this.
And that is when a realization has dawned to you making you no
longer the person you used to be....
From now on, everything has changed,
Changed forever with a never return clause staring at you.....

-Arati Harikumar

IT'LL BE ALRIGHT

Under this bare blue sky, I wanna look into your eyes

Hold your hand and let you know

Your abundance is as much as that sky

Your circumstances aren't you.

Your fears don't define you.

Like the little welcoming Orange amidst the blue,

So is life, a little cold and a little warm.

You could still hold it,

Close to you, with all the love within you.

There are times when the same sun that makes you shine will make

sure your wounds burn.

But again, the cold nights will soothe your wounds.

There will be nights that seem long and you'll wait for the morning.

There's nothing bad, there's a balance.

And someday you'll be calm inside and shine on the outside. Very

soon.

My promise to you.

-Sanyogita Bharadwaj

DELICATE FLOWER

Fragile to touch
Wisps of air
Blowing it away.
Floating up high
Touching the sky
Back down again

Crumbling to pieces
Dust it turns
Stem left behind.

-Maria Wynnyckyj

ENOUGH

a guided touch
across the sky –

the silhouette of
a simpler time.

the moon, still here,
has yet to give up –

but our earth, I fear,
has had enough.

-Sarah Kordos

THE UNFINISHED LOVE

She remembers his rusty scent
That still burns her heart,
She remembers his gray songs
That still flutters her heart,
She remembers his weary shoulders
That still wraps her heart,
She remembers his unpolished smile
That still crushes her heart,
She remembers,
The unfinished love.

-Pooja Shroff

MOONLIGHT

The moonlight guides my path tonight
I pray somehow it remembers the route that will lead me to you

I walk past trees and rocks marked by age as the sweet air fills my
lungs drawing me closer though you be so far away

Oh! Make me a promise dear lover, that you will wait for me as I
journey across plains and seas to be with you

-Frances Abhulimen

THAT LITTLE BIT OF WILD

she was that little bit of wild
that could never be tamed –

that dare to Love kind

who's not afraid
of a one-way lane.

-Sarah Kordos

AS HER STORY WROTE HER

she wrote her story,
as her story wrote her.

each letter –
of her past.
each word –
of her future.

every moment she wanted to relive
and each moment she wanted to erase.

her cure, her tormentor –
her embodying pen.

her soft as silk paper.

she wrote her own story –
and her story wrote her.

-Sarah Kordos

SOLITUDE

it's true
that you
hide away from the sun –

but it's this cold
that will burn
you till you're gone.

-Sarah Kordos

HIDDEN

I can't switch it on and off like you,
I can't force a smile when my eyes tell the truth.

I can't ignore the moments that cut me deep
because they're always there – just like the air.

and they try to keep
me in the ground,

away from all the sounds
of joy –

of music playing
without bounds.

my scars aren't there for you to see
but hidden deep inside of me.

-Sarah Kordos

WITH A ROSE

with a rose,
I used to see the rose –
but now, I just see petals.

their colours used to make me feel
but now, they're just dark
and red.

I find myself drawn to the thorns,
and I touched them gently –
but still I bled.

-Sarah Kordos

THE TRUTH IS

the truth is
I don't own you

(although I wish that you were mine)

and even though I want it,
it may never be our time.

-Sarah Kordos

SOMETHING MORE

and I hope for life
when I am dead –
I hope to see what has not been.

I hope to feel
like it all meant
something more than what was said.

and when the moon
lives on and on,
I hope she too has something more

to look upon.

-Sarah Kordos

WHAT WAS

I felt at peace
when you were with me,

as though I had a cause.

I ignored the truth –
that we could never be.

and now, we're just what was.

-Sarah Kordos

DISTANT

it's different on this side,
it's different in this mind;

there's chaos then there's order –
a storm on top still water.

a surface so calm, but distant,

that you'll never get the chance to know
what goes on beneath the show.

-Sarah Kordos

MOON

In the gloomy night,
Under your distressing light,
I stood there alone,
Waiting for you like a stone.
I remember the daylight,
When you were losing your might.
I can still recall the sigh,
When you were about to die.
My heart was calling your name,
As the morning stood by.

-Affan Alam

CONTROL, A MYTH

Control is a human arrogance, and myth
not allowing one to live in the moment of their day....
Always living in tomorrow and planning
not savouring daily blessings, in a blessed way....

The Raven does not store, nor does it want....
The Lilies of the field neither toil nor spin.
Yet God let's each day be a blessing, of that day they're in....

Do plan for your tomorrows
but live and enjoy the one you're in.
Control is just a myth, and arrogance is the sin....

-Afreen Fatima

QUEEN OF HEARTS

Once I had a game of cards with grandpa,
And told him how the world has evolved into a competition...
With the encapsulation of all the struggle and the rage,
If you wither you'll always have a substitution...

He patted my shoulder with his wrinkled hand and said,
"My child you're never a part of THIS struggle...
When you focus on your dreams,
You must replenish every single drop of sweat with smiles and
jiggles...

Future is just a string of some mysterious stories,
Which has been knotted to your NOW...
Ignite yourself for what YOU DREAM,
Because my dear 'competition' is just a hypnotic game anyhow!

Sit sometimes in front of a mirror and ask yourself,
'Am I on the right shelf of books?'...
People will always keep talking the fictions,
But do you really deserve hanging over their hooks?"...

Shallow as I was,
I kept figuring out his absurd words to reach the core...
Watching me he tossed the Queen he held and said,
"One day, you'll stand out like her I'm sure"...

And today?
Shiver runs down my spine when I remember those deep words in his
soothing voice imprinting on my thoughts...

I'm thankful to you grandpa for those worthy words,
I miss your presence every time I hold that Queen of hearts...
I badly miss your presence every time I hold that QUEEN OF
HEARTS!!

-Khushi Thakare

PILE OF MIRT

You're the unseen morning light.
You're the beautiful bright night.
Whom I'm gonna miss throughout my life,
Despite it is not a scar of knife.

You may not be seen,
But when I glaze at your pic,
My-my life seems a beautiful trick.
You're the peeping rays,
Of a beautiful sunny day.

But I have to let you lose,
Cause you're just a blooming rose.
If it is as true as virtue
Your presence would be due.
If it is not,
It still is a lot.

-Affan Alam

REMISSION

My soul has been in starvation
So I come to you seeking salvation
I don't know if this is my pre-emption
I'm only here asking for redemption
I only want to rid of my anguish
So I ask, please make this vanquish
I want to put my life in the clear
I want my pain to disappear

I want to restart the ignition
Show the world my own definition
To be able to follow my own intuition
I only want to put my pain in remission

I need to have my mind vindicated
Enter this new life fully translated
Time of my past, it's time to omit
Enter this change I must commit
It's time to see myself ascent
Rid myself of all this torment
I want to put my life in the clear
I want my pain to disappear

I want to restart the ignition
Show the world my own definition
To be able to follow my own intuition
I only want to put my pain in remission

-C.L. Williams

FIRST RAIN

She is like the first droplets of rain,
Soothing away the heaviness of the pain;
(Pure as a lil baby's smile yet insane)
She is the sound of the drizzle after a long sunny season,
Gives a hope that every yearning has a reason;
She is like the cool breeze after a mist,
A sense of happiness but with a twist;
She is the smell of mud after the first rain fell,
Couldn't deny but accept being under her spell.

-Jagruthi Kommuri

QUARANTINED

Last night,
I climbed in my train with a relieved sensation,
I was on my way for an unexpected vacation.
I my compartment was an old man with a mask,
sitting at the window along with a huge cask.
Answering to his smile I asked him if he was a cooper,
patting the cask, he said, "No child, I'm a Tutor."
Analysing my confounded expression,
He said that was his profession.
"Here in the cask are the luxuries of billions,
I snatched away to teach them the importance of their pavilions.
Here in the cask is the freedom of society,
which I've quarantined to make them learn the lessons of unity.
But these frivolous students of mine take it as a vacation,
silly students don't know it is an inevitable catastrophe for their

nation.
They just take it flippantly, injudicious of their actions,
they must know the voice of the suffering ones are not just

animations.
Still I give them a chance to confront their incognizance,
and if they win I'll pour back the cask of their relevance."
Shiver ran down my spine as an aura developed behind his glowing

face,
I woke up with a sudden haze.

I looked at the clock and was late for my train,

But the old man of my dreams surely gave me some brain.

This is not self-quarantine, instead this is self-care-before-we-are-out-of-time.

And just another lesson from God for us, that dilemmas don't know what is the discriminating line...

That dilemmas never know what is the discriminating line...

-Khushi Thakare

ARE YOU AFRAID?

Are you afraid?
So am I.

Watching the world shatter.
All searching for their ruptured pieces,
With erratic minds and maniacal laughter.
Thirsty for shelter underneath a shadow,
Or portraying someone they wish they could be.
Pebble by pebble making the water rise,
Till the dart hits reality.
Are you afraid?
So am I.

Of these crippling souls with bleeding notions.
Empty minds not responding the bodies,
Now straining the thoughts to stop the collisions.
They smile with the blue,
They wither with the black.
The present is at the stake,
For the future to never collapse.
Are you afraid?
So am I.

Of the life which left us numb.
But hold on..we reside under the same skies,
Believe that somehow the blissful days are always to come.
Are you afraid?
So am I.

So are we.
But one day, life's gonna agree.

-Khushi Thakare

WHY

What is life to feel it a competition..
Why do we see not the awe of great creation..?
What is that we ever thirst..
Why do we never rest..?
What is weakness to not feel..
Why is strength seen as a great deal..?
When love is something that helps us grow and believe..
Why do we still hold on to hate and leave..?
Do we not know everything is nothing yet just for a moment
illusions..
Nevertheless, we are always in search of some infinite conclusions!!

-Jagruthi Kommuri

YOUR EYES

While everyone saw the universe with their eyes,
I could perceive the same universe in your eyes;
While everyone was hiding words in their eyes they never want to
reveal,
I could read the poetry in your eyes that you wanted someone to find
and feel;
While everyone was merely looking at each other who are near,
I could see the depth your eyes hold for someone very dear;
While everyone who search yet find nothing nice,
I could find the eternity in just a blink of your eyes..

-Jagruthi Kommuri

YOU

I search for you in every person I meet,
Isn't it funny how one person can make you feel complete;
You were the distance I wouldn't mind to walk,
My journey with you will forever be special to talk;
Each new day you seem to be a new story,
I would like to read and unveil the glory;
You are somewhere miles away yet very near,
Why is love so strange to express and hence I fear;
You might think you are just like any other person one can find,
I want you to know that you are one in a million kind;
Words could limit in describing what you mean to me,
But I hope someday you will definitely see.

-Jagruthi Kommuri

HOPE

Hope, because it keeps us going,
Hope, because it helps us growing.

It doesn't make things easy,
But it sure does make you believe the impossible,
And you know what, hope will one day make things possible;
It will test your faith at times,
But it is what that brings us together,
Hope gives us courage to help each other;
It will one day challenge love,
At times when you are drowning in doubt,
And you'll know hope is what made you try it out;
It may seem like everyone is changing,
And everything around you is falling apart,
Then hope is the only thing that aids in surviving till last;

Hope, because it makes life worth living.
Hope, because it helps us keep trying.

-Jagruthi Kommuri

CONFUSED SOUL

When we are kids we want to grow fast,
When we are young we wish if we could last,
And in old age we sit and regret our past;
When we are single we wait to mingle,
When we are in love we wish be to single;
We don't know why our hearts flutter and tingle;
When we have nothing, we wish we had something,
When we have something, we wish we had everything,
But someday we'll know everything is nothing;
We wish we had chance to choose,
Sometimes we gain nothing but lose,
Yet this restless soul is left confused.

-Jagruthi Kommuri

I AM ANGRY

I am angry that you only need me for cuddles and milk.

I am angry when you don't open your mouth when I try to feed your meal.

I am angry when you reject the special dish I tried from those fancy forums.

I am angry when you poop just when I start my meal.

I am angry I never get to drink my coffee hot.

I am angry because you don't give me some time to catch up on my insta feeds.

I am angry I can't watch my shows as you watch your cartoons.

I am angry I can't get enough sleep because you like to play as and whenever.

I am angry I can't get into my old but cute tops and my jeans don't fit.

I am angry you gel so well with your nanny and don't miss me the whole day.

I am just angry and angry and angry. Husshhhhh....

But now that my baby you slept, and I gaze at your face. I feel sorry...

It's not your need but you want me and my cuddles, it comforts
you like you were in the womb.
You may be teething and might be in pain so don't want that
food.
You were already full after the feeding session a while ago and
might not be hungry.
You are just too small for that bowel control.
I feel sorry it's a phase and every single second of it will pass away
forever.
You won't me this tiny always.
You don't eat my food now but might serve me the best of
delicacies one day.
You would be strong enough to take your decisions and
judgements without needing those soft cuddles.
I may have all the time to myself, but you won't be around
screaming for a hug.
I might just see you through your insta feeds.
I will have all the time to rest, eat and sleep but your cozy warmth
next to me won't be there.
However well you get along with your nanny, you jump at the
sight of me entering our house and crawl towards me, your speed
faster than yesterday. That welcome gesture will also be gone in a
few days.
All my body fat would be gone, but that's the rent you paid to
stay within me for 9 months and I will be losing that as well.
Every minute I am losing some element, but I promise this will be
fresh in my mind always.

I wish I could lock this time and keep you small, but you will have
to grow.
I pray you become a gentleman, a sensible grown up but trust me
I dread that day.
You may leave our nest and flyaway to touch the high skies.
Just remember we will still love you and you will be the same new
baby always.

But now
I am angry again, please wake up and play with me again.

-Namita Das

DIVINE SIGN

I look at the moon, it reminds me of your serene face,
Just as it lights up the night, you ignite my darkest space.

I look at the stars, they remind me of your sparkling eyes,
Just as they twinkle and befriend the lonely sky, you help me
illuminate and empathize.

I look at the sun, it reminds me of your angelic smile,
Just as it warms a winter morning, you make life's adventures
worthwhile

I look at the flying birds, they remind me of your wavy hair,
Just as they flutter by and bring joy, when you are around, love is in
the air.

I look at the roaring ocean, it reminds me of your melodious voice,
Just as it gives solace to the soul, you have become my heart's rejoice.

I look at this vast universe, every detail of God's marvellous design,
While everything reminds me of you, every lil thing about You
reminds me of God, cause I believe you are his Divine Sign.

-Jagruthi Kommuri

TAKE ME AWAY

Take me away miles and miles,
From this cruel world and those fake smiles..
Take me somewhere with no humans around,
Just hand me my books and heal my wounds..
Take me to the oceans and the sandy beaches,
Where every wave sounds calm without any grudges..
Take me to the mirrors who see the perfect in me,
With no one to judge on my goofing; setting me free..

But you can't, right?

Then take me where I find some true guys,
Where money speaks less and talent doesn't sighs...
Take me where love genuinely becomes strength,
To such an era where I start trusting the word 'friends'..
Take me where I shape my own features,
No hammering by parents and dumping of teachers...
Take me where this world of my imagination exists,
Where every morning is blithe with elegant nights to assist...

But you can't, right?

Then take me away miles and miles,

From this evenly cruel world and those weirdly fake smiles...

-Khushi Thakare

LIFE GOES ON

This moment, it soon becomes a memory,

Recapture happy times before you understand life is temporary;

A friend someday might become a stranger,

Don't let love end because of a minute's anger;

Your grief will one day be healed,

Your lie, it definitely gets revealed;

People like seasons may change,

Be yourself, let world assume you're strange;

Present will become future's history,

Life even till the last breath is a mystery;

Today will become tomorrow's yesterday,

Learn to Live, Love and Laugh anyway.

-Jagruthi Kommuri

ALL THAT EXISTS

Every loss is someone's gain,
And when you think nothing is left,
Remember you are left with pain;

Every pain holds a story to tell,
And when you learn to accept it,
you will defeat every rival so well;

Every beginning has an end,
And when it seems like it's the edge,
you will find it is just a bend;

Every bend holds something good & new,
And when you finally do what is due,
you'll see bravest like you are only few;

So embrace every loss, pain and twist,
One day everything will end, all that exist.

-Jagruthi Kommuri

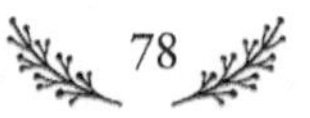

TO THE FULL

a pull towards what makes me whole –
a tethered rope that won't let go.

it doesn't matter how hard I try
to break away – a strong divide;

the waxing crescent to the full,
the moon creates my strongest pull.

for whatever reason, I don't know why,
she's there for me, she gives me life.

-Sarah Kordos

DEAR FRIEND

I met someone,
so different, but alike
we shared,
our talks and our thoughts,
our mysteries and our stories,
our laughs and our cries,
our tears and our joy,
our fights and our abuses,
and yes,
I got a precious friend,
eventually,
life played its part,
like every stories,
we parted,
distant by hearts,
affections left in wane,
talks lessened by time,
leaving back our memories,
ages afar,
I'll remember,
our promises and dreams,
that left trauma and grief within us,
but still saves a bit of love and care
deep down the heart,

whispering,
what a wonderful friend I had
dear one....

-Dr. Apteena Johnson Kakkadu

THE DREAM CATCHERS

They come to you, when you need them the most
Asleep, wide awake or in trance
They seem far but familiar and seem wise
At times quiet, other times, they make some noise
Yet they manage to shake your being
Make you question your existence
In the course, they give power or wings
They let you be in a fantasy world
Bereft of reality but allowing trust and means
Or they will push you into despising reality
Living in dreams is no mean feat
And living out of it is no feat at all
The trick is to balance fantasy and real
And build a bridge across, long or short
And travel from dream, toward it, encompass it
And strive to make them happen
To make it tangible, visible
What happens next?
Do you see more or is this it?
That's the brutality of real world
It kills your dreams!

-Rajlakshmi Kurup

WHAT DO YOU DO WITH A STRONG WOMAN?

What do you do with a strong woman?
The one who is free spirited and kind and beautiful
The one who you are afraid of because the light in her
shines brighter than any lamp you have ever seen

What do you do with a strong, kind woman?
The kind that has set herself free from any obligations
For her kindness arises from strength
And you don't know what she is made of

You don't know what to do with a woman like that. I
understand.
So, you kill her spirit, you break her wings. You think you can
tame her
You believe that dousing her fire will quieten her
Alas my dear, how can you douse the fire that is raging in her

How can you quieten the sparkle that shines so bright

How will you ever tame something that you cannot fathom, let
alone handle?

Pray tell me how.

-Arati Harikumar

DEPARTURES

Departures are the hardest, especially when it's long distance love.

The warm hugs again turn in hugs in a frame...

The long talks holding each other's hand turns into calls between
breaks

The good night sleep in each other's arms turns into video calls till
sleep

The intense kisses that took over a heartbeat turns into virtual lifeless
kiss.

The little mischiefs that brought smiles turns into call pranks

Just in a moment the entirely grown realistic love withers back to the
virtual love

Yes, departure gives you pain, agony and disturbed mind,

But it also leaves back memories to be cherished and love to be
nurtured

Long distance is hard it can bring lot of thoughts and doubts

But if you survive this phase you survive all the hurdles towards
victorious love

-Ashwini Pandit

BLANK PAGE

A normal day

Just the time past lunch

The sun somewhere between over the head and the west

I sat near the window

Looking at the lane

I took out my book

Storming my brain

Trying to write a poem

I wrote a few words

Stroked them off

Repeated the same

Looking at that blank page

I started to fear

I wanted to write

But nothing seemed right

I closed my eyes

Took a deep breath

I opened them

I saw the sun,

bright and loud

Fiery and proud

I turned the page

And I wrote this down

Without striking out words

My hand running with the flow of my thoughts
And that's when
I understood the fact of life
That there is a heartfelt poem waiting for you
After every blank page!

-Pravallika Kadiri

LONGING PATH

I walked and I walked again
a path that flourish our memories,
The grass used to dance,
The petals used to swirl,
The path used to smile,
The bedding full of flowers,
We used to walk.
The tree veils our laugh,
The path remembers our encounters,
The day I saw you,
The day I met you,
The night full of your fragrance,
The flower that resembles your smile,
The eyes that warms my soul,
The scent of you disappeared,
I try to catch you in a long starry night,
My love that slips away,
I try to fly to you,
My love,
Do you remember?
The sun that let us see through our shadows,
The moon that let us see through our souls,
The path that brought us together,
The wind that took me to your heart,

The path that longs for you,
My reflection in lake longs for you,
The path and I walk together,
In a hope to meet you again

-Pooja Shroff

YESTERDAY'S DIARY

I keep you dear to my heart,

I keep you safe in my ink,

I write you every day in my song,

You smile between the pages of my "yesterday's diary".

Underneath the moonlight,

While listening to careless whisper,

I write about our first coffee,

I write about your smile,

I write about your eyes,

I write about your tears,

I write about you in my dreams,

I write about our first snow,

Writing about you became my happy hour,

My swaying destiny,

The person I forgot,

Your memories that faded away,

My yesterday's diary remembers,

Her folded curls,

Her faded ink,

Her old dates,

My letters to your heart,

Stayed in my "yesterday's diary".

-Pooja Shroff

WHAT DEFINES A WOMAN IN THE 21ST CENTURY

She must cook
She must earn
She must be educated
She must 'act responsibly'
She must prove her worth by managing her job and her house

She is not to delegate her responsibilities
She must not wear clothes that bring 'shame to her family'
She must ensure that the family, neighbours, and their extended
neighbours have a good opinion of her
She must not raise her voice
She must not socialize

She must not drink
She must not smoke
She must not 'attract attention'
She must get married irrespective if she wants to or not
She must sustain the marriage even if it has no meaning for her

She must ensure her uterus is used and the bleeding stop for 9
months
But the bleeding of her heart continues for another 90 years
She must also ensure that the child of her will be a male
She must then ensure that she brings up a fair man.
HOW?
And lastly, when will you tell her that she should stop breathing?

-Arati Harikumar

ALL LEAVES FALL

Coloured in rich red
And aged bronze,
I had already left.
My soft wood had no use,
I had grown old with the immortal sky.
I lay waste on the ground,
Such a life has gone by.
My brothers lay beside me,
It has been a long night.
The mighty wind has shown mercy;
Fates have such unparallel might.
No wonder then that today, again,
Our mother tree
Has to watch our deaths go by.

-Anushree Gupta

In this War, Without You

Every morning without you makes me weak,
And every night it gets harder to sleep,

The scorching heat reminds me of your cool eyes,
And the lonely afternoons, of the painful goodbyes,

I imagine you caressing my hair,
Shooing away my nightmares,

In this war against humanity,
We maintain distance to preserve our sanity,

Oh, how much I want to be with you,
To love you, without caring about the invisible enemy.

-Snehal Agarwal

LET'S MOVE ON

Again, after a long time, I got a chance to hug on my favourite couch.
It always throws me in a deep well of thoughts, I can't come out of it.
I am trying hard, but I am strangled, the more I try tighter the
strangles get.
Get me out of here, please.

In the journey to success, I left many people behind.
Call me selfish, I don't mind.
I would continue the path I chose.
Some I really wanted to hold on, but they could not come with me,
had a different journey fate decided for them.

Still, I question, why did you abandon me? What was my mistake?
I grew for you, but you are still not happy.
You taught me to climb but when I did, why don't you join me?
You had a choice; you made a choice.
I was treated like one of the options that once rejected you.

I am heartbroken, left with scars.
I have no one to talk to, because I would not let you down.
You walked over me. I want to finish it off, the pain is unbearable.

I smile but my heart weeps. I want to shout, cry out loud.
I want my answers, but my calls are uninvited.

Time to decide, stick-on, or move on.
I decide to leave you behind.
Go. Live your life, but do not hesitate to callout if you need.
I pray you never need to.
I must choose now. I choose to go ahead on the journey.
I choose to be successful. I choose to shop. I choose to party.
I choose the ones who value me. I choose to live.
I choose to be happy.

My brain is jammed with plans, but my heart was left empty.
I choose to give time. I choose to fill it with love from genuine lovers.

I wish myself the best of everything. Goodbye bad memories and
welcome a new ME.

-Namita Das

YOU

When you push me to the edge of my tolerance
It hurts me but I stand there strong.

Your silent attacks made my heart shallow
But still you can't prove me wrong.

When you turned the worst eye on me, that pricked like heat strokes
Ahh... I am burnt, my skin is scaly,
I am crying for help but my throat choked.

And one fine day I was touched by a pure soul,
Beautiful heart worth much more than gold.

A burst out of emotions and overnight of tears down poured.
That was a night of realisation, it's my heart, a house of sentiments.
I will now decide which one gets it the longer to rent.

The night of downfall is followed by a bloom of colours and
freshness,

I am up and revived now, cheerful and fearless.

When you strived and thrived, convinced me and all, I was a dead
loser.
Carefully I replaced this YOU as I wish to spend the rest of my life a
happy bloomer.

P.S. Choose wisely, who you want to be surrounded with.

-Namita Das

IS BREAKING

it's hard to show emotion,
I really don't know why
it's hard for me to express
the truth I feel inside.

I wish I could harness
the power of my mind,
I wish I could just focus
on my own personal design.

if only I could know
what drives me every day,
instead of simply living –
then maybe I wouldn't stray.

because I find myself daily
losing pieces of my soul,
I find myself living plainly
every day without a goal.

nothing keeps me motivated
and I quickly get frustrated,
which in turn keeps me isolated
from a life I wish to lead.

and the speed that I am taking
to create a life to live
is breaking
every ounce of individuality
in me.

-Sarah Kordos

DID I BID YOU FAREWELL?

The city that never sleeps, the city that never let me sleep, the
place that kept me on my toes.
The friends who always had my back, the family which has been
my pillar.

The temple carvings that know my deepest fears,
The tranquillity the sea has offered unconditionally.
The familiar routes and places, the gawking hawkers to the
helpful strangers.

The taxi drivers who have seen me shed many a tear
The places where memories are created, the alleys where games
were played.

The nosy neighbours and the accommodating maids.
The watchful eyes of family and friends, the playfulness of
childhood companions.

The rebukes and the fights with the near and dear.

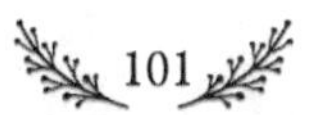

The pillows where dreams were shared, the long nights where
secrets were exchanged.
The promises when broken and hearts were then shattered.

The long walks lost in my thoughts but knowing the route home,
The feeling of being lost but knowing that I am not.....
Did I really bid you a fine farewell, my city of unabashed hopes
and dreams?

-Arati Harikumar

MEET THE CO-AUTHORS

Bhavya Rao

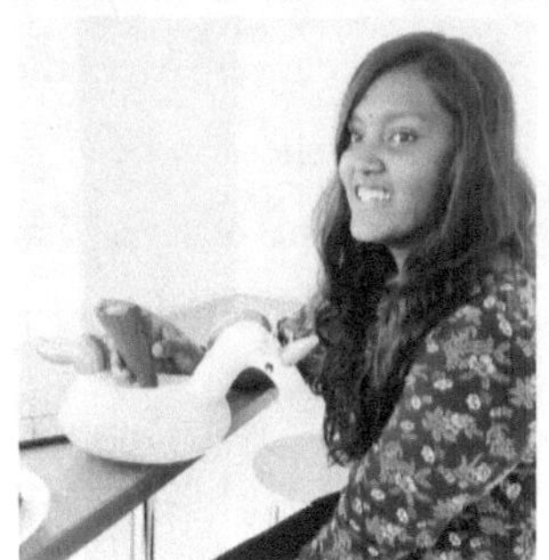

Bhavya is a 20-year-old business student with a curious mind trying to witness art in everything possible. She believes that connecting metaphors to reality is an escape.

Sarah Kordos

Sarah, born in Canada, started writing at an early age and has only recently begun to share her poetry with an audience. She is a lover of love and hopes to convey that in her poetry. Sarah's empathic writing ability takes her poetry through the vastness of human  emotion, drawing inspiration from both her own experiences and her surroundings.

Arati Harikumar

Arati Harikumar is a passionate Human Resources professional working with Deloitte India. She relentlessly pursues many hobbies - a reader by day and writer by night, a dancer over the weekend and traveller when a destination beckons. She believes that there is so much to explore and experience in life and one must never stop learning. A quote by Voltaire "Writing is the painting of the voice" sums up what she feels about writing - she is on a journey of finding her voice with every tale she spins.

Sree Yelamanchi

Sree is a doctor by profession and writer by passion. She chose writing to get through the dark days of her life, and eventually fell in love with it and that is when she started to believe that "It's not you that choose writing, but it's writing that chooses you". Books, coffee, and chocolates are her aesthetics and she plans to live the rest of her life taking it as and how it comes, just one day at a time.

Sneha Hembram

Sneha was born & brought up in the 'city of joy', Kolkata. She hails from 'steel city' Jamshedpur, and has graduated in English Honours from Ravenshaw University, Cuttack, Odisha. She then pursued post-graduation in Fashion Management  Studies (FMS) from National Institute of Fashion Technology (NIFT), Kolkata, West Bengal. She loves writing during her spare time, expressing her thoughts & emotions through words. You can check out her other pieces of work at her Instagram *@whispers_of_soul_sh*

Sanyogita Bharadwaj

 Sanyogita Bharadwaj is currently pursuing Bachelor of Arts in Psychology, Journalism and Literature. *The Love I Know* & *Hope and Beyond* are her published works. She's an aspiring psychologist. She believes - "Be it a battle with yourself or the world, no matter how big or small, love and a little more love is just enough to conquer."

Pooja Shroff

She is a person of Letters and pages. She lives in her little fairy forest of flowers and ink. She is a savvy and brilliant writer who creates her books of poems and stories from her mystic world of Four Seasons, The Moon, The Wind, The Stars and The Meadows.

Amol Gawade

Amol Gawade From Dahisar, Mumbai. Civil Engineer by profession, humanity is a religion for him. He shares his positive thoughts through his Instagram @amulyavichaar. He believes in karma, and looks forward to positive things, better days. For him, "You get in life what you have the courage to experience."

Arubah Nadeem

Arubah Nadeem is currently pursuing a degree in B.A Psychology, Journalism and Literature in Hyderabad. Born and brought up in Jeddah, Saudi Arabia. She is a firm believer in helping others irrespective of what day she has had.
She believes "Words tend to give people hope again in their life".

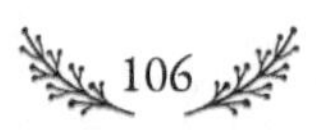

Kunika Rawlani

Kunika Rawlani originally resides in Ulhasnagar, Maharashtra. Currently, she is pursuing her CA. Writing is a dearest friend of her which she got to realise one and a half years ago. She never gets tired of writing, thinking, and sleeping.

Frances Abhulimen

Frances Abhulimen, a Nigerian lawyer who also writes under the pen name Frances IsiBoro, ventured into creative writing in 2019. Some of her poems have been published by Eve Poetry magazine, Poetry Nation and PoetryNook magazines while one of her short stories is being considered for a movie in Nigeria.

Affan Alam

Affan is a high-school student, who is very much attracted to English language and literature. He also likes non-fiction and composes short tales and poems from a noticeably young age.

Maria Wynnyckyj

Maria works at a state college and is a writer and amateur photographer. Eventually, she aspires to get her work published. She is a proud mother of three grown children and two grandchildren. Maria currently resides in the USA. Maria is inspired by art in all its forms because of what it reveals to her. She has a rather funny and twisted sense of humour that comes out when she is comfortable with people.

Afreen Fatima

Afreen is a student in Hyderabad. She is an avid reader and likes to write on a regular basis and is fond of music. More than provocation or eliciting an emotional response from the reader, it is her personal therapy that she seeks through poetry. Being an introvert in

social surroundings, and an extrovert in musings, her ambiversion finds a balance in words. Emotions expressed via artistic medium make the joy and suffering of humanity a uniform and common ground for association. Her passion is peace and love, and she is in the pursuit of simple happiness. She describes herself as a lone wolf, she doesn't seek special attention and social engagements. She believes, "every memory is a metaphor, and every person is a poem."

Jagruthi Kommuri

K. Jagruthi is a B.com E-commerce graduate who loves to write to ignite a little hope in the reader. She's a simple girl who finds solace in words and writes to spread love & positivity to the world. She believes kindness goes a long way if communicated through heart.

Dr. Apteena Johnson Kakkadu

She is a 23-year-old dentist as well as an aspiring writer. She started her writing career with her debut book- Lord of the words vol-1. She always loved to scribble down notes about her feelings and perspectives. She strongly believes that her writings would reflect and influence people's hearts and minds. Her writings are mostly based on women empowerment which is encouraging as well as strengthening. She also believes that healing is the utmost strength and moving on as a new being is the superior power of the soul.

Rajlakshmi Kurup

Rajlakshmi Kurup works as a freelance writer. She loves writing fiction, mainly short stories, and poems but she also dabbles in non-fiction opinion pieces when inspiration beckons. Her writings have been published in several online and print publications. She lives in Navi Mumbai.

Priyanka Ravi Nair

Priyanka Ravi Nair is a 24-year-old MBA graduate in Finance from Pune. She found her passion for writing more than two years ago and there has been no looking back since. She has featured in various anthologies in the past and is going to turn editor for her next book "Three Bodies One Soul".

Pravallika Kadiri

A 19-year-old management student who likes her thoughts to be on a paper than in her mind either by writing or painting. Pravallika believes that everything in this world happens for a reason. One might find it difficult to understand her because she has a realistic approach towards life, but at times she can be an emotional baggage too.

C.L. Williams

C.L. Williams is an International Bestselling Author living in Central Virginia. He's written eight poetry books, five novellas, one novel, and is a contributor to a multitude of anthologies. His previous poetry book The Paradox Complex features the poem "Sad Crying Clown" that was turned into a short film by Matthew Mark Hunter of MMH Productions and is available to watch on the MMH Productions' YouTube channel. He is currently releasing a series of novelettes under the banner Chaos Fusion. C.L. Williams is currently working on his newest poetry book OMNI- and Bed Bugs, a supplement book to the MMH productions film of the same name.

Anushree Gupta

Anushree Gupta is a high school student. Reading being an addictive hobby, she fell in love with the way of words which brought to her the world of writing. When she isn't reading, writing, or listening to music, she finds herself lost in her textbooks or cycling outside with her friends under the sparkling summer sun.

Ashwini Pandit

A professor by profession, poet by passion, she loves to spread love through poetry. An enchantress for her students and someone who can be contagious. According to her, words can express what actions can't. She's a person who is full of fun and smiles. You can follow her on Instagram @the_sassy_poet

Snehal Agarwal

Snehal Agarwal is a 21-year-old Chartered Accountant from Mumbai. She is talkative, a sitcom fanatic and secretly a nerd. Writing allows her to explore, acknowledge, and accept the problems persisting in the world and she believes in making a change, one day at a time.

Khushi Thakare

Being 17, Khushi is extremely fervent about discovering more of herself with the formative years. She believes that writing is just another form of telepathy & besides academics the lanes that you pursue immensely alter your thoughts. She has co-authored the book "Little

Occult Affairs" by Inkfeathers which is a compilation of mysterious & thriller fiction.

Namita Das

Namita Das is an engineer who wandered into writing codes, but her heart was always set on writing creatively. She is a frequent blogger which centres around humour. A quick visit to her blog "Pen It Rather Key It" is a kind of stress buster and keeps readers abreast with the latest happenings.

Tanvi Kulkarni

Writing is not just a passion but a modicum of bringing change in our world. Believing this, Tanvi Kulkarni, writes out her heart and the earnest feelings in it honestly. She believes that no topic is too risky, too cliché, too deep or too light to write about. That being said, one of the reasons why she started writing is feeling the rush of ink and scratch of the pencil on the paper. Even you, fellow readers, know about the enamouring smell and feel of paper. Reading a lot of classical literature, wonderful world of fantasy, facts that bring to light the state of our world made Tanvi involuntarily start to write. Hoping to entice the readers with her strongly felt and lovingly worded creations for a long time.

OUR STORY

We're all on a Journey, and our "Writers" have made it Beautiful.

A dreamcatcher is an object made with feathers and strings, essentially used as lucky charms in many parts of the world. The same way, Inkfeathers brings together writers, editors, and artists together to form a dreamcatcher that works in favour for the young writers and readers and if you're positive about it, it may bring you luck as well. We at Inkfeathers are connected to thousands of writers globally, who believe in the magic of telling stories. This stream of connectivity with the writers, the fact that everyone has a unique detail or edge to their story makes Inkfeathers proud to partner with these young literary as well as collaborative minds.

Back in 2013, our founders came together to form an offline group for their love of literature, and this formed collaborative energy with many young literature-wounded minds which eventually led these offline meetings to stand-ups, storytelling events, poetry slams, meet-ups to share experiences and many others. In 2016, Inkfeathers finally launched as the brand project under one Private Limited Company. This expanded opportunity gave a number of possibilities and a new way to expand our support for writers.

This dream of wanting to bring together writers as well as readers has come true beyond measure as writers connect to us from countries like United States, United Kingdom, Canada each day to bring their stories to life.

As of this year, we are extremely delighted to provide you our website (www.inkfeathers.com) where all your queries can be resolved about our self-publishing process and latest anthologies. You can get hold of the latest updates on anthologies, events, offers, new book releases and so much more here. You can go ahead and order a book from our bookstore to get a taste of our mindful curation of stories and poems. Inkfeathers Publishing family encourages you to really put your feelings out there in words for the world to see, in order to have a common ground to grow mutually. We are a creative platform for all those seeking literary help in terms of having their words published.

Believe us, publishing a book is not easy, but we come to a writer's rescue at each phase of having their book in print in terms of Editing, Designing, Branding, Marketing and all the other work that goes behind until you have a printed copy in your hands for Distribution. Together, it couldn't have been any easier. We will be there for you, to help you turn your manuscript into a freshly bound book that sells off the glass bookshelves.

With Love,
Inkfeathers Publishing

OTHER PUBLISHED BOOKS

Hope and Beyond brings some stories of warriors; some real, some fictional who fought an unseen battle, not with a living monster but with something more powerful, our own mind and body. The world is closing and what is most important is to open up to yourself and to have faith in the warm hugs you receive on your way. This book wants to test that power of sharing and test the strength in the stories of acknowledging the heavy and hazy days.

**Scan the QR Code
To know more & order your
copy.**

Taking you on some unplanned, mystical journeys into this realm of 23 beautifully mysterious minds. Little Occult Affairs has everything it takes to keep you flipping through pages trying to envisage each writer's mind and experience life, death, secrets, darkness and so much more as you dive deep in it, making you feel like you live the story itself.

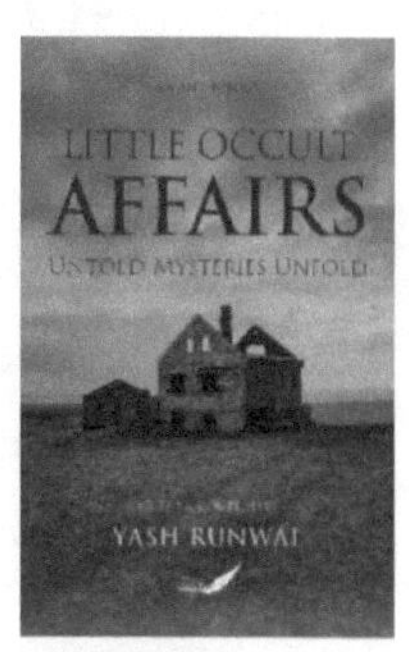

**Scan the QR Code
To know more & order your
copy.**

Forgetting the hustle-bustle of the regular world, let's dive inside a deeper realm that has so many intriguing mysteries to offer. Our heart has a lot to teach us. This book will open your mind towards the untravelled purpose, the undetected significance and the unexplored value which lies within us and around us. LET THE HEART LEAD has everything it takes to make you acknowledge the spirituality that resides in all of our hearts. From "Self Ishq" to "Spirituality", from Spirit Animals to Resonance and from soul mates to twin flames, this book has it all.

**Scan the QR Code
To know more & order your
copy.**

Do you feel stuck in your own life? Are you going through the same motions and call it living? Have you lost your joy and desperately crave for much-needed seclusion from everything around? Behest by the malaise of hustle and chaos of big cities, Midnight Writers offers you peace in solitude, a beautiful way to embrace silence. This anthology of poems has familiar and unfamiliar terms and phrases, some modern, some long, and others freshly minted.

**Scan the QR Code
To know more & order your
copy.**

Wouldn't we love it if life was just fun and frolic? Unfortunately, life isn't idealistic. For some, it might be just a living hell. We all are here to play certain roles, but some turn out to be players. What might appear on the outside may not be entirely true. Their facade is so realistic that we can't see through and there are stories we wish weren't true. This book contains 19 such stories which belong to different genres like supernatural, contemporary fiction, horror, romance, thriller, sci-fi to suit everyone's taste.

Scan the QR Code
To know more & order your
copy.

Ready to embark on a journey? From the fields of historic wars to tales of fantastic warriors. The common man stuck in the play of cosmos. The love so well cherished by the people of the past. The new light that shines as the dust over our mythology and history blows away. Are you ready to see the new light yet? The Forgotten Sagas is the ticket to this journey of yours. Through a mixture of poems and stories, it transports you not only to different parts of the world but also to the different eras seen by the human race. The extraordinary tales and verses will not fail to keep you entertained and will leave you smiling to yourself.

Scan the QR Code
To know more & order your
copy.

INKFEATHERS PUBLISHING

India's Most Author Friendly Publishing House

Stay updated about latest anthologies, events, exclusive offers, contests, product giveaways and other things that we do to support authors.

 Inkfeathers Publishing

 @InkfeathersPublishing

 @_Inkfeathers

 @Inkfeathers

 Inkfeathers.com

We'd love to connect with you!